# PREFACE

Katrina Hidalgo, unlike most visitors to Tafesilafa'i, rode in on a limousine with an entourage to rival that of any Hollywood celebrity. She was the marketing agent for one of our guest speakers that year. In Los Angeles, this is not uncommon, but unlike many Hollywood celebrities, Katrina came and stayed with our community. Katrina saw something in the Pacific Islander community that touched her. She participated in our meaning making exercises and rituals over the years and since that ride in 1999, Katrina has re-invented herself and weaved into her life such a Pacific Islander thread, that she has found the strength to put her healing story on paper for the very first time.

One of Robert Louis Stevenson's character in Treasure Island was inspired by his friend William Earnest Henley who said, though he was covered by the night, "black as the Pit from pole to pole," he gives thanks to God for his "unconquerable soul." And though his head is bloody, he is "unbowed" and "unafraid" because he knows he is the master of his fate and the captain of his soul.

Katrina knew from her mother and family that she is the master of her fate and captain of her soul, not her teachers, friends, doctors, money and the "powers" that be. Katrina also knew that for her to come out of the night that covered her, she must be "unbowed," "unafraid" and "unconquerable."

This work is a testament to those characters that Katrina so exemplify which makes her "unconquerable." It is a testament to her will to live, her love of life and her courage in the face of overwhelming odds. I pray that her story inspires you as it has many of us.

Peace and Blessings


Misi Pouena Tagaloa

# I Survived

## by: Katrina Hidalgo

I am finally telling my story in hopes someone will find the courage to do what we did and win the battle you are fighting.

## Ask questions, it's your body!

CIN-1?? What the heck is that? Abnormal what?

Is this another part of Epstein Barr Virus?

Can I have a copy of that please?

I went straight to my mom's office. I showed her the papers and asked what they meant.

She said she didn't really know for sure but would make a call. Well, after a phone call my mom made to an M.D. friend of hers, I could see in her face it wasn't good. After being what I called the "nuprin poster child," I was not expecting what was about to happen.

I knew I had pain so it couldn't be cancer. You always hear the old story of "cancer is the silent killer." When she told me what it meant, I about fell face first on the floor. How could this happen?

My first thought was, "this is not going to be the

end of me no matter what!" I am not accepting that word into my mind or my body. I'm about to become a grandmother, I need to be here to welcome him/her into this world. That baby became my main focus. Forget my photography studio, my modeling shoots, trying to be "someone."

I was on a mission for information on how to handle this demon without the options I was facing, in which we've all heard the words, Chemotherapy and Radiation.

Well, why would you give me radiation when every time I go to the dentist they put this huge blanket on my whole body so that "radiation" won't damage me? It's just an X-ray on my tooth. Why would you put something in my veins that would burn them? This was NOT an option!

My mom always told us, "Your body will heal itself and if you really need a medical doctor then see one." My mom had never even been to a doctor herself, except to have us kids, as I remember. She's a natural healer and believes in a Higher Power for everything except when we kids would fight and end up needing stitches. She did take us to the medical doctors. I remember her saying words like migraines and gout or something like that but she never took pills or even aspirin and neither did we.

I remember being at Loma Linda Hospital in California and my doctor was the head of Oncology. He had an open mind. I knew God sent me to the right place and the right person. He told me we would just "wait and watch" and let me pretty much take control of my treatment. So now my journey began.

We both agreed in the beginning we would never use that word Cancer. I was going to use my mind to defeat this and I didn't want that word in it. He totally understood and agreed and thought it was a great idea. We always used the word "sick" until the day he told me I was now Cancer Free. I believe you need a team of professionals in this condition. Get as many opinions as you can before making your final decisions. I actually had 3.

First stop was the American Cancer Society to see what they could offer me as far as help. I had always donated to that organization and I just KNEW they could give me the right information to help me on my journey so with all the hope in the world I walked into that office and for the first time I admitted I had the dreaded "C" word...Cervical Cancer.

I was expecting a group of people to come out and hug me and tell me everything would be ok, there were treatments or something, anything that would help on my journey of hope. After all, I had donated to them so much, in the hopes that someday if I needed them, I could go and get help.

Well, the American Cancer Society was not what I nor my husband expected. The lady behind the desk was very cold. She said that the A.C.S. does not help people with cancer...they are a research organization!

**Well, What the HELL??**

After my having a fit, she offered me some information on my type of cancer and printed something off the computer that I could have gotten myself without the humiliation. I asked her if there was ANYTHING they could do for me as far as help with funds because I wasn't able to afford the treatments I wanted. Any organization you can point us to for help? She explained if I needed hospice care in "THE END" I could contact them again and they would give me a real nice bed and free oxygen. Oh gawd. Here we go, there's those words...IN THE END??

We both just left and sat in the car for a bit to digest what had just happened. We knew we were alone. There was no one to help except the medical field that wanted to fill me with poison. I had never met anyone at that time who was a Survivor who wasn't all messed up somewhere else from the chemo and radiation.

NEXT!

That was my exact thought.

NEXT!

One of my sisters had always been into natural medicine and lived in quite a few countries that only used naturopathic medicine.  I had no clue about it or what it was.  I just knew she was weird because she never went to the regular doctor and my niece could not eat the foods we ate.  Hmmm, she must be one of those "vegetarian" kinds of people, is all I ever thought.  No biggie, everyone is different. But they never really got sick. They never had to go to that medical doctor.

One day, soon after I went through my first major crisis she came over to my house with the most beautiful gift basket I had ever seen.  She told me they were essential oils and she wanted to teach me and my husband how to use them to get me on my path to healing.  Well, that wasn't accepted too well since I knew nothing about them and actually didn't have time to listen. I was on a mission to find my own "cure."  She took the basket home with the saddest and oddest look on her face. She never gave up.

Next thing I know, she tells me she wants me to go to a seminar in San Diego and just listen, keep an open mind about Aromatherapy and Essential Oils. Mind you, in 1995-96 not many people had even heard of those things. Okay, Okay, she's my sister. I guess I should at least give her a chance and get some information.

*This* is the changing point in my whole life, not just with my cancer.

When we got to the convention, it was at a beautiful hotel. The food they served was organic something I had never even seen before and there wasn't much of it at all. It was mostly vegetables and fancy lettuce. "Oh geeez...here's those vegetarian people again," is what I thought.

First I met Gus who had invited my sister, and then I met his twin brother Chris. Both were the most gentle and kind people I had met so far that day. They were from the East Coast so their accent cracked me up. I remember that much and being twins made it worse, double trouble. Chris was there along with me for knowledge. His brother Gus was a distributor and a very strong one too, strong in his convictions that Young Living Essential Oils could help me. He never asked me to pay for anything or buy anything and neither did my sister.

Ok, now my ears were buzzing, I had to know what these special oils were and why they could help me. I was ready to give it a shot. Everyone began to fill the room and I was seated second row from the front.

Somehow I got separated from my sister and began to have a major panic attack. The people surrounding me had already purchased their oils and had them in their purses or pockets. Some were rubbing **lavender** on my forehead and neck. I remember one lady offering me a cup of water with a drop of **lavender** in it. Well, what the heck, I'll drink it. I'm with doctors so if I pass out they will CPR me. I started to feel a little calmer immediately and my heart began to slow down from the race it was in and my stomach stopped feeling like I was going to throw up. (*make note to self...**lavender** vs. Xanax*)

Gary Young had taken the stage and I tried to pull myself together enough to listen. I remember my sister sitting in the row in front of me with Gus and Chris but she kept looking back to make sure I was okay and smiling like "its okay sissy, you'll be fine."

Gary began to talk about **aromatherapy** and how it gets into the cellular level and can actually change the way they (the cells) react to certain viruses and infections. That day is the day I learned Cancer is a VIRUS !! This man had just explained in about 20 minutes MORE than the American Cancer Society did. Now he's got my attention.

I started writing notes, never even noticing my panic attack was completely gone. The note I did write to myself and still have to this day in my book is: *"Success in life is like baking your own cake. You have to try different ingredients and measurements over and over adding a little of this, a little of that, taking out or exchanging this or that until you find the perfect recipe for your own self. Then you can share your secrets with others and they can mix their own recipe and so on and so on."*

I guess now is the time for me to share my secrets and recipes with you.

My favorite and most important oils are highlighted within this story. Most are being associated with the situation I was dealing with at the time.

The whole lobby smelt of so many different fragrances, I remember thinking maybe my sister isn't crazy after all. Most of you probably have heard of that "white light moment" when people swear they saw the brightest white light and were given a message? Well, I didn't actually 100% fully think that was possible unless you were Moses or Sister Theresa until that day in Escondido, California.

Gary Young was talking about I don't know what, then all of a sudden he began walking to the side of the stage I was sitting on, and I promise you I SAW the white light surround him and he was almost floating. I doubt anyone other than me saw him in that light at that moment but I know I did. I've seen that light before but just not under these circumstances.

He started talking about his new oil **SARA**. I remember him explaining how people who were abused would get the most benefit from the oil or something similar to those words. Those are the words I remember. He talked about sexual abuse and other abuse as a child and how the *"inner child"* needed to be healed before the *"grown up"* can move forward. He was looking me straight in the eyes as if he knew why I was there, even though he had no clue of who I was. You needed to **Release** the trauma from your memories. Okay...where did this man come from? At this point, here I go wailing out in tears, everyone around me knew it was some sort of "moment" and were again rubbing *lavender* on my forehead, massaging my hands and I just knew something was about to happen.

Well at that point nothing did. He finished talking about **SARA** and ***White Angelica***. The white light went away and now he walked back to the center of the stage talking about other oils. I knew I had to get that **SARA**. I knew what had happened to me and I knew what was being said was true. It's just not as easy as he said, was what I thought.

After the seminar I pretty much ran to the lobby where the beautiful displays of oils were. I found **SARA**!! OMG what was going to happen if I really did smell it? Could they be telling the truth about some oil that you can actually smell that can possibly help erase or remove ugly memories? I don't know but at this point, if I was told to eat dirt I probably would have, so here goes: I close my eyes. Take 3 deep whiffs of **SARA**, breathing slowly in and out like they told me to. I was facing the table and was not paying attention to the crowd that had gathered in the lobby, I was "in my moment." I suddenly felt what I thought to be a few fingers running down my spine. My first thought was: "turn around and nut the person who is touching me during my moment." (Truth) I didn't kick him but I did turn around and for a brief moment and **F L A S H**... I saw my grandfather's face in that MAN who had just run his fingers down my spine. I turned back around so fast and started smelling that oil, praying that this was not some sort of cult situation I had just stumbled upon, and when I turned back around to face reality, that man didn't look like my grandfather at all.

He was the kindest-looking older gentleman. I know he knew he startled me. I will forever remember he told me he was a doctor of this type of medicine and offered to take me to Hawaii to heal me. There were more words exchanged and a few hugs. I do not remember his name nor did I take him up on his offer but right then I knew I was in the hands of where I belonged. I was hooked. Could **SARA** be real? I have thought so, from that moment on.

Gary and Mary Young were being bombarded by the press and I stood there long enough, maybe 20 minutes or so, and I needed to see this man and his wife no matter what.

Well, I was told no one gets private 1 on 1 with Gary Young or Mary Young and I was like, "excuse me, I'm here on a mission and I will see him" so I and my sister, along with Chris, just pulled back the ropes, kind of took both of them by the hand, opened those huge conference doors and walked in alone and shut the doors on the press and the lobby. Remember, I am on a mission. Both were a little amazed and I suspect a little tickled at what we had just done but I explained I had cervical cancer and I was there for him to help me.

He explained he's not "GOD." HE could not heal me. Well duh ...I knew that. But I also knew I was sent there and he had the message I needed from a human, a natural doctor, a person who had the knowledge that I was not able to get from the American Cancer Society.

He asked if I had my diagnosis papers and I gave them to him. He and Mary looked at them and both sort of smiled like "oh she's going to be fine," gave me a hug and proceeded to tell me all the oils I could start using along with some other information about how to use them. Neither one of them said it was a "cure." Neither one of them tried to sell me anything. Wouldn't have worked at that point because my sister had everything they had. Neither of them told me to stop seeing my medical doctors. In fact, both said not to stop with my medical doctors and see if they were open to my new options.

I didn't ask why but I was overwhelmed with this whole day and Chris started writing down what Gary Young was saying so I got it right. **Lavender, Joy, SARA, Valor, the whole Essential 7 kit and Ylang Ylang** were the first group of oils I started to use. I remember the words "turkey baster" and about fell on my face!  "OMG he did not just say that in front of some man I don't even know." Well yes he did. Mary was cracking up with my sister about how shy I was.

Chris and I are still friends along with Don, a noted sports personality.  Mary is the kindest woman I met during the beginning of my journey.  Her hugs were warm and heart felt.  Neither one of them was "blowing smoke" to try to sell me anything.  Both were genuinely concerned and I feel blessed I was able to get my 1 on 1.

Chris and my sister were able to get some of that special attention too, ending the day with everyone feeling satisfied with the knowledge we were leaving with. Chris is a kick boxer and wanted something for bone pain.  He was told to use **Birch and Pane Away** to start with. Every time I hear someone say they have bone pain I immediately say "use birch oil."

A few of my favorite oils still to this day are: **Ylang Ylang, Valor, Peace and Calming, Jasmine, Orange and Wild Tansy**. I mix and match them to come up with my own blends for my own purposes.  I wouldn't recommend this to someone who hasn't used them before.

**True Essential Oils are very powerful.  If**

***you are allergic to certain plants you will more than likely be allergic to the oil.*** You need to really take the time to learn about the oils before using them. Perfume oils are not the same and will not work at all for medicinal purposes; this is what I discovered to be true for me. I have tried several oils and several brands.

As we went back into the lobby there were a few tables set up to sell some of the oils and the new ***Progessence cream***. Never having a clue that this product would play a major role in my later decisions I bought a few jars and was asked to help behind the table. I felt honored and gladly accepted. I later learned the seminar was set up by the group that had invited me, so I was happy to have helped.

I remember a few months later I received a call and was asked, "Who did you tell the people to make the checks out to?" I said, "Ted Baker." He said, "Are you sure"? I said, "Pretty sure, why?"

Well, I was obviously on cloud nine or something from my new-found experience with essential oils and aromatherapy because I actually told quite a few of them to write the checks to Ted Bundy. Yes, you read it right, Ted Bundy. Now I knew why the people were looking at me so oddly, asking "are you sure?" when told to write their checks

17

payable to: Ted Bundy.  Maybe I should have smelled **Lemon**?  I laugh every time I think about that part of my journey.

Shortly thereafter this group went to Oklahoma to bring oils and help the people affected by the Federal Building bombing.  Young Living associates are special people who are always willing to share the knowledge with everyone and anyone no matter rich or poor, sick or healthy, believer or not.

I received 2 books titled "Aromatherapy the Essential Beginning."  One Mary signed for me (during our private meeting) and I keep that one special but the other one was for my "notes."

When I signed up for my auto-ship so I didn't run out of the oils I wanted, amazingly I got # 25,000.  Everyone on the YL side was excited since they were waiting to see who got that number.  I was excited too because 25 is a lucky number for me. My goal at the time was not to sell the product but to learn as much as I could so I could heal myself emotionally and physically, then spread the word and let the oils sell themselves.

I read that book cover to cover and, back then, I could almost tell someone about aromatherapy word for word via Gary Young's book.  I was so intrigued that our medical doctors had no clue about what I was talking about, but in other countries aromatherapy is very widely used to treat conditions for which here in the States we use poison instead.

I asked my doctor at Loma Linda if I could use these oils and would they hurt me? He said, "They will not hurt you and you can use them if you want, it's your body and I'm here to help you." I just loved my doctor and knew he was not going to try to convince me anymore to use that chemotherapy or radiation.

I had gone earlier in the day for my "tour" to show me what the chemo room looked like and how comfortable it is. Shaking my head the whole time, I knew I was not going to do it and when the nurse took me into the room I saw 2 women sitting at machines. Yes, I agree, the chairs did look comfortable, a table with an apple was visible, and both women had their backs to the door reading a book, with beautiful scarves on their heads.

The nurse acted like she was showing me around to buy a house or car or something. I was rather offended. She asked me what I thought and I said, "I still think the same way I did when you asked me last time. The answer is still no."

"Do you see my hair"? I asked in a stern voice. I pulled it from behind my back and it was down to my hips. "This is me...this is who I am. *This is my identity.* If I do "go out" anytime soon, I'm going out with my hair. Do you get it?" She then proceeded to tell me I was the vainest woman she had ever met and I said, "I'll be back in 10 years with my hair!"

I had read in my book that anointing oils were in the Bible. I started looking deeper in the Bible to see for myself. I used the index since I'm not a scriptural person.

Let me tell you something. There are so many references to the oils in the Bible and what they are used for—more than in most references you can buy online or in a book store. It's amazing and you don't have to be scriptural to understand it. I'm not and I got it real quick and kept reading as many as I could. I'll leave that up to you to research if you feel the need or desire. Even if you don't agree with the Bible, look at it as a history book and just research and read the parts about the oils. ***Frankincense, Lavender and Purification*** are a must for all households. Read as much as you can about essential oils. There are a lot of references online.

Every night my husband rubbed my oils in my feet. My sons would rub them on my hands. My boys would carry ***lemon oil*** in their pockets daily. I told everyone I knew about these oils and how they were going to heal me enough to beat my cancer. The oils I used every night were **Lavender, Joy, Peace and Calming, and Valor**. I would use other oils also or at the same time but those I just named were the ones I used all the time. **Ylang Ylang and Jasmine** were an almost daily routine. I kept **Jasmine** on a cotton ball in my car. I heard **Rose** oil also was very healing.

We noticed about a week into the massages my husband's wart— or whatever it was that he had for years— was starting to go away. That thing would never go away no matter what OTC medicine we tried, but the oils above in combination removed it completely, no scar, can't even tell it was there. I don't know exactly which oil it was, or if a blend of a few did it, but it's gone still to this day and the wart has never come back.

I never thought they would cure me. I knew they were a key to something I didn't yet know, but I knew they would be a huge part in my survival.

A lot of my friends were scared. They kept explaining that everyone they knew in the world (not literally) who had cancer and survived was because of the chemo and radiation. I kept hearing if I didn't hurry up and get started it's going to spread and I won't have a chance.

"Oh, great!" Now I decided it's got to become personal and a journey on my own. Hardly anyone understood the risk I was taking because I didn't get it yet. That saying, "fear of the unknown" is pretty powerful if you let that "C" word get a hold of your mind or others around you. Their fear will get into you and you have to stay strong for yourself. You don't need to explain anything to anyone. It's your body! I had to take control and learn everything I could. Luckily I had wonderful Medical Doctors.

My sister was a huge help. I finally started to listen and learn about the Vita-Flex and Raindrop massage techniques. In my opinion Vita Flex and Raindrop therapy is the next best thing to chocolate.

Time went on and I went back for my appointments and things were changing. Some were good, some bad. Good ones were: my immune system seemed to be getting stronger. Bad thing was: the cells were still out of control. Ok, so, let's just give me a little more "watch and wait" time and see what I can do.

I was diagnosed with Hashimoto's Thyroid Disease at the same time so I knew that might have something to do with the crazy tests.

I started using more oils, changed my diet somewhat to that "vegetarian" thing I was so afraid of and the sun started shining again. I wasn't so fatigued, I had a better appetite and I wasn't losing weight. I asked about surgery and was told it is always an **option** but most people opt not to have it and instead use the traditional chemo and radiation first. "Are you kidding me?" I asked.

After many discussions and descriptions of what would happen if I had a radical surgery, I told him I wanted surgery to get the crazy cells out. He agreed and they did a procedure, not a total procedure, but removed what there was of those cells.

The good thing was, I had been using the oils and building my immune system and my body was strong enough to handle a surgical procedure. I actually started feeling better, had more energy but still wanted more information. My Loma Linda doctor was amazed at how well I was doing and my attitude of "not giving in." We had agreed in the beginning never to use the word Cancer, and we called it "still sick." I knew if I just had a virus, then I could beat it if I did what I was reading and what I was told. I always considered both my medical physicians and others in the "natural" world's opinions. I never felt odd or weird asking questions. After all, they are the doctors. I never had one medical doctor who was not willing to take the time to explain anything I wanted to ask about. I would suggest you look and look for a doctor like that if you don't already have one. They are out there!

As time went on I would talk to my regular doctor and discuss my options with the oncologist and I decided to get a total hysterectomy.

I was tired of all the appointments and wanted to just get it over with and get the cells and tumors out of me. I was losing weight again and getting fatigued pretty easily at this point but my immune system was pretty good and my skin was healthy and the rest of me was pretty healthy and my grandson was here now and I just wanted to start living again and stop thinking about the virus.

### *Choosing the surgery.*

By now I had enough knowledge to know: get the cells out, keep refusing chemo and radiation and I'll make it. When any disease is serious and you have a major surgery they take you in a room, tell you to get all your "eggs in a basket." I mean, dang, how scary is that? My eggs will be in a basket all right, a casket basket along with my ovaries and tubes!

This was a major decision because in the past I have had bleeding issues and they said I would be in surgery about 4 hours. Usually I would donate blood before operations in case I started bleeding out. I asked if they could please use my **lavender** oil immediately after the staples and **helichrysum** oil if I was to bleed out. This was discussed prior to the surgery, and as long as it was sterile there was no problem so I brought them along. I was told I would have to take hormones the rest of my life because everything would be removed. Well, again, that's not an option because I had already geared up with my knowledge of the oils and supplements and **Progessence**!

Let's get this show on the road and be sure NOT to give me any hormone shots before I wake up. I've got my own bag of tricks ready for me in my room.

Surgery took a lot longer than expected, about 6 ½ hours, because of a few complications but it was all removed and then some, just like I asked. While I was out, they kept taking pieces and sending them to the lab until the pieces came back negative and then took a little past that. I guess this is the normal procedure for that type of surgery.

I woke up in my room and just like I asked, I had **lavender** on my staples, 38 to be exact. I was in the room no longer than a few hours when nurses started coming in and wondering what smelled so beautiful. I said, "It's my **lavender** oil." Before I left that hospital 5 days later, I had shown almost every nurse in the oncology ward all the oils I had and showed them the book and told them how I used the oils to keep my hair. I had them in a beautiful velvet bag with a gold tie.

I was massaging half the floor before I left. It felt so good, not only to know I was more healthy than ever in my life but that I was able to share with a whole field of medical professionals about the oils.

I'm pretty sure Loma Linda uses Aromatherapy and Essential Oils at this time. I've seen on T.V. the commercials of the Cancer Treatment Centers in Tulsa Oklahoma and it says they use this type of therapy.

I have twice donated my hair to the "Locks of Love," always asking if they can place a note with my hair saying, *"it's from a survivor so it's good luck hair."* If you cut your hair and it's of the right length you can donate yours, too. Just search for them online and they will tell you how to send them your hair, or talk to your stylist. You'll feel so much better seeing your hair go into a bag, knowing it's going to someone who has none, rather than seeing it being swept up off the floor in the trash.

I still have days that it's impossible to talk about being "sick" and what all I went through. It seems like a dream. If the records weren't there I would have to wonder.

I have days I feel so bad for being a survivor and wonder, why me? Why not that other lady with all those kids who was about to be a new grandma?

Most days I'm happy to wake up and can't wait to share my knowledge about oils and supplements and aromatherapy.

OK, so years go by, I'm still cancer free, no chemo, no radiation, against most odds, and the best thing of all for me is my hair is still down to my hips and that grandbaby was a boy. He was almost as beautiful as my son the day he was born. He is my little (not so little now) earth angel. The reason I wanted to survive.

In 2010 my husband's regular blood work came back odd. His doctor asked him to retake it. He did. Obviously something wasn't right because he was asked to take another series of tests a few weeks later. We thought he was eating something wrong before the tests so that had to be it. He was diagnosed with Prostate Cancer stage 2. He didn't show the "regular" symptoms but he was losing weight and had a lot of fatigue. We were told on our 35th anniversary, Valentine's Day. It sort of ruined the mood.

Here we go again, but this time we know the road. We've traveled the path before. The genes you were born with you have to deal with.

Find the best oncologist who believes in Natural Medicine and— lo and behold—one call from our primary care doctor and we found him. Just as easy as I found everyone I needed, we found someone for my husband.

Our new Oncologist was impressed with the fact that all my husband wanted to know is if he had the "operation" how long would it be before he could get back out on the golf course. When asked that question I think the doc was in shock. I assume most people that are told they have cancer start crying, falling on the floor like I did but no, he wanted to know how long after the operation it would take to play golf!

Again we were told about "watch and wait." Let's not use that word please. No chemo and radiation. We prefer not to allow that into our heads. He agreed. My husband's level at this point was only about 12. We weren't terribly excited because we knew we had a few numbers to go before we needed to go into "high gear."

This time around was different; it was my husband. Now I got to feel what everyone else felt about me, the being afraid, the sadness, the "what ifs." I began asking his Oncologist could we try what I had tried with my cancer. To our amazement, he was happy we even knew about all that. He said he welcomed it. Between him and our regular doctor I knew my husband would be okay.

We immediately started treatment with oils and supplements. An N.P.D. in Seattle was sending him boxes of powders and pills. I had to trust someone else this time around because I had stopped using YL. He was using several supplements but the Fractionated Pectin Powder was so nasty he actually had to use hot chocolate to mix it with. Nothing else would work. He did this daily along with a strict diet but not leaving out his favorite foods.

I believe when your body is already in stress, don't freak it out more by totally going organic or vegan if you don't know how to substitute the food. I taught my husband about visualization, one of the techniques I used, and he immediately took to it and was able to do it in a few days. He couldn't use my "Pac man" method but he came up with his own.

He believes in aliens, so he visualized that tumor was full of aliens. He visualized the mother ship above his body pulling all the aliens back up into it and killing them. The aliens were actually the cancer cells themselves in his visualization technique. For whatever reason, this worked for him.

It also helps give you a visual for meditation which relaxes your body.  Either way visualization is a good thing in everyday life.

Luckily for us, we understand that our primary care doctor and specialists are there FOR us and we are allowed to, and expected to, ask as many questions as we have.  If any of our doctors would have had a bad attitude or attitude of "do as I say or you will die," we would have walked out. You should, too, in my opinion if that happens to you.

I'm not sure why they always want to start with the poison. Why not start with the obvious?  What exactly is that "wait and watch" thing if it's not for you to research your own disease? There are more of those doctors out there than you know.

My husband being diabetic, we knew he really had to be in the best shape he could be because we already knew the only option for him would be surgery.  No chemo, no radiation, no trials and he needed to get on that golf course as soon as possible. Just get as healthy as you can to be able to handle a major surgery was what we decided to do. Cancer does have symptoms and fatigue is a big one. At least for both of us it was. His numbers went up to almost

30 in just a few months. We decided it was time. The Oncologist explained to us that his type of cancer was "aggressive." We knew what my husband was facing. We had done all the research. Learned all about Lupron Hell and everything else negative about having a radical surgery. None of those "side effects" have happened to him and he's back on the course with his sons and grandson.

A few days before his scheduled surgery, my nephew, who had just turned 18 and visited us earlier, was found overdosed in a local hotel. He had just told us he would be at the hospital on Tuesday for his uncle's surgery. Teens having a "hotel party"!

My mind went numb. What was I supposed to do? My mind and body wanted to shut down. I had helped raise my nephew many of his years. My sister had struggled so hard as a single mother to keep her boys together and I had just failed her. I had to be strong. I had to not lose it. My husband's surgery was in two days. I tried in my mind to pretend my nephew's death was all a dream and not a pre-curser to my husband's surgery, but ugly thoughts took over and I was in a total panic state and shock, and I think I literally lost my mind. Where is that **lavender and joy**? Don't show any sadness. Don't show you want to just die. Keep strong for your husband because he has a major surgery. Tuesday, hurry up and get here.

Tuesday finally came, everything was ready to go, they wheeled my husband down the hall for the first surgery of his life and all I could do was wait. Wait like he did all those times alone in that family room for me. Wait and pray that the doctor would come out of those doors with a smile on his face. Wait in the chapel praying for my nephew, trying not to lose it because my husband needed me now more than ever. You're really never alone in those rooms; family is usually with you but in your mind, you are alone with your thoughts.

It had only been a little over an hour. I expected about 3-4 hours so I sat in the chapel praying. My sister came in and a chaplain spoke with us. I told him she had just lost her son. I was trying so hard to be strong.

Someone came to tell me my husband was in the recovery room. I wondered where the heck is the doctor and why didn't he talk to me. It didn't really matter because "recovery room" was the best words I could have heard. Good or bad, he made it through a major surgery. He slept comfortably through the afternoon and night and tolerated some food. The tumor was successfully removed in record time.

I just know there was some huge football game

on the next night and that's all my husband was worried about. Not about where his meds were, not about pain, not about getting out, but where the heck is that "man cave"? I need to see the game. I asked several nurses in the ward if there was a private lounge that might have ESPN so he could watch the game. We were told no. I laughed. Anyway, he was feeling so good and it's only a few hours after surgery. Poor guy was about to have withdrawals.

I decided that we should just head on down to the cafeteria since he felt so good. Maybe, just maybe we can find some man cave. He got out of bed with no problem, grabbed the IV pole and away we went. I was actually amazed because he had his stomach cut from top to bottom, not side to side. I have had both and that one was worse for me but he acted like it was nothing at all. We got to the elevator and he wasn't dizzy and walked down one very long hall, then another one and got to the cafeteria.

Little did we know, his doctor was there to see him. He had walked into the room and patient was nowhere to be found. Find him! Okay, so the cafeteria said we can't come in because he was too soon out of surgery and we went back up to the room. After I explained to the doctor about the game, he was laughing and could not even believe my husband was out of bed. He was asking "how do you feel?" and "why did you get out of bed so soon"?  I snitched and told him my husband needed to watch that game.  He already knew my husband was a sports freak because the first words were "when can I hit the course"?

Then the doctor told us that the surgery was one of his best ever.  He had done hundreds before and no one ever acted like my husband.  He said when he opened him up it was as if there was a road map for him to cut on, that's why it didn't  take any time at all.

My husband explained he had very little pain and wanted to go home now, he needed to watch that game.  Not sure how, but that game ended up on his T.V. in his room so he was a happy camper.

We understand that most men leave the hospital about 4-5 days after this type of surgery.  He went home on the 3rd day, walking with no problem at all and having no post-surgery complications.

It's been almost 2 years for him now since the surgery and he's doing great.  Our Oncologist said he's going to use my husband as an example in his seminars as to how they need to start changing the way men are expected to recover after prostate surgery.

Although Young Living Oils were not used on

my husband, the supplements he used did contain most of the same plant extracts.

I wanted to share our stories now because I feel it's time.

Neither one of us claims that essential oils from Young Living or any other company cured us. We are not saying any supplements from Young Living or any other company cured us. Who knows if we are "cured"?

Right now, I know we are both cancer free and living quality lives.

I do not take hormonal supplements. I refused from day one after my surgery.

**My question was:** *"How can you expect me to take a little yellow pill and tell me it comes from the pee of a pregnant horse and expect me to swallow it?"*

There are so many ways to help your own body help itself. You just have to start your own journey and find them.

Now I'm getting back into my oils. I should have never stopped them. Just like most medicines, when the immediate danger is over, we tend to just go back to our old ways. I want my Young Living oils back because they are the only things that really work without causing other issues with my health. The ones I prefer to use are my own personal choice. Whatever blends I choose to make or use are my own personal choice and preference from experience.

I will say with all honesty and heart, and have said for the last 15 years: Gary Young and his wife Mary opened a whole new world for me through Young Living Essential Oils which I believe enabled me to obtain the knowledge I needed to say I am a Cancer Survivor Today. Neither of them promised me anything. I would love to meet with them again someday to say thank you.

I just hope with my story you will know that there is truly something else out there besides the poison we are prescribed daily. More often than not, whatever issue you are dealing with today you can trace it back to the beginning and it will all stem from some sort of trauma that is keeping you from moving forward. Remember my story in the beginning? I told you about that table with **SARA**? I was also told before I smelled it to be ready to **"release the garbage from the past."** I believe that to be the most powerful statement I've heard in my life, even to this day. Thank you, Chris.

Good luck on your journey and have fun while

you are learning.

Don't take someone else's knowledge as a threat against you but embrace it as a gift sent to you to increase the library in your mind.


**Knowledge is power take as much as you can get.**


I am now on a new journey. I have been the Coordinator for the Tafesilafa'i Pacific Islander Festival at the Aquarium in Long Beach for over 10 years, winning 3 awards for Religious Organizations. I can't wait to see where this leads me at this stage in my life. I feel so blessed to be a part of this culture and this year our theme is healing.

I believe the timing is perfect for me to share my story so I too can begin healing once again with my Young Living Essential Oils. It's been many years for me and I see there are so many new products. Now I will learn about those. I want everyone I know and will meet in the future to know that Essential Oils and Aromatherapy are a very vital part of our lives, and the more we know, the better we can be. You don't have to go flip-flop or anything crazy. Start slowly and learn each essential oil one at a time.

I would suggest finding the one that makes you feel the best and start with that one. The Young Living Essential Oils Essential 7 kit was a great place to start for me. Nothing in that kit is too overwhelming to understand and you will be surprised at how much you will use it every day on things you can't imagine right now.

One thing I have learned over the years through research and working with people who have been abused is that your memory is the key to all things both good and bad and smells are almost always associated with them.

Another thing I will tell you is until I was about 35 years old I would never allow coffee to be brewed in my home nor did I drink it. Now I love the smell of my fresh brewed coffee in the morning.

The more you learn about Aromatherapy and things in your past, the easier it will be to move forward and be successful in whatever it is you are choosing to conquer.

I can say for sure, until you get rid of the garbage you can never fill that space with happiness and love.

Sit back and relax.

Listen for the rain drops. Get to a quiet spot in your

mind and enjoy the never ending possibilities once you take your first smell of true essential oils.

Listen for your messages. They will come when your mind is finally quiet.   With Love   ~ Katrina ~

Photography by my sister Traci Metzger  Vacation 2011

www.tafesilafai.org

www.ingramcontent.com/pod-product-compliance
Lightning Source LLC
LaVergne TN
LVHW021549080426
835509LV00019B/2918